A souvenir guide

Mr Straw's House
Nottinghamshire

Andrew Barber

National Trust

Meet the Straws

Mr Straw's House is the quintessence of Edwardian success. It bears the hallmarks of social ambition, with modish decoration and up-to-the minute conveniences, including electricity and indoor plumbing.

The house proclaims the success of a family that had moved from living 'above the shop' in the busy Market Place, to a semi-detached home in fashionable Blyth Grove, an exclusive private road set above the town centre.

The Straws were a family that valued commercial skill, hard work and academic endeavour, and sought to reflect their new social status through their home. While no expenditure was wasted, neither was any spared in perfecting it to Florence Straw's taste. In the socially fluid environment of the early 20th century, this is what success looked like.

Yet the survival of this Edwardian dream is far from typical. Established in the aftermath of the First World War, Endcliffe Villa's refined domesticity might have withered in the face of economic depression and a renewed energy for 'the house beautiful'. That the surging self-confidence and ever-changing fashions of this age of consumerism didn't seem to affect Endcliffe Villa is down to William and Florence Straw's two sons.

Keeping the status quo

Ingrained with a love for the status quo, as well as the shopkeeper's respect for economy, neither boy saw the need for any modifications. As the world around them changed with accelerating vigour, William and Walter Straw carried on as they always had done.

William lived to be 92. Had he died 20, or even ten years earlier, it is likely his family's legacy would not have survived. As it is, in 1991 the National Trust saw the value in Mr Straw's House as a social document of increasing rarity. Emboldened by its evident national importance, the Trust took the brave step to save it. Meet the Straws: not hoarders, nor recluses – not even very odd – just people of their time, long after their time had passed.

Left Blyth Grove, a private road north of the centre of Worksop, was developed as a series of speculative and private commissions from 1900

Right William Straw, with his sons William and Walter, outside the family shop in c.1902

William Straw

William Straw was born in 1864 in Sutton-in-Ashfield, Nottinghamshire, where his family was established in the manufacture of earthenware. William, a younger son, was apprenticed to a Mansfield grocer, William Pegg, in 1880. With his elder brother Benjamin, he moved to Worksop to start a grocery business in 1886, with £700 borrowed from family. Three years later, William bought his brother out and ran the business alone, selling not only groceries but also items from his family's pottery business.

William was an active member of the Worksop Traders' Association, and was elected President in 1898 and 1921. By 1903 the shop was doing so well that he was able to buy the building, together with two adjacent inns and the yard behind, which came with several cottages. During these early years he lived in the flat above the shop. In 1896 he married Florence, the daughter of a prominent Worksop tradesman called David Winks, whose butcher's shop on the corner of the Market Place was opposite the Straw's. The pair had three children, William (born 1898), Walter (born 1899) and David (born 1901).

William had an acute financial mind, working in his spare time as a trustee of the Grocers' Association and the Worksop Savings Bank. He dabbled in the stock market and enjoyed picking up bargains at local house sales. He also loved gardening, a passion inherited by his sons.

Right **William Straw Sr**

William added a flower and vegetable seed business to his grocery enterprise in 1898, a part of the business expanded by Walter when he joined his father in the shop in 1919.

William was a dutiful husband and loving father, corresponding almost every day with his wife when she went on holiday, either to the Yorkshire coast or with her parents to the spa at Askern near Doncaster.

In 1932, at the age of 67, William died of a cerebral haemorrhage whilst stooping to tend a plant. It is perhaps poetic that this happened at his allotment in the 'Gentlemen's Gardens' off Sparken Hill, just south of the Market Square, a place where he had spent many happy hours.

Accidental damages

In November 1899, William defended a claim for £21 damages for injuries sustained when a boy was hit by one of William's carts. Witnesses described the boy running out in front of the cart, and the impossibility of the driver stopping in time. However, the judgement went against William and he had to pay the expenses of his witnesses, his solicitor's fee, plus £5 of the requested sum in damages. Following the dispute, William was moved to create a 'Traders' Defence Fund' after one of his witnesses wrote about the injustice of the situation in a letter: 'You have the satisfaction of telling the truth and of honesty having prompted you to defend the case … You have the knowledge you fought on the right side, if might was on the other.' The fund was set up with the backing of the Worksop Traders' Association.

Top left **William Straw, the boy on the left**, served his apprenticeship at Pegg & Sons, a grocery shop in Mansfield

Bottom left **The cover of a shop calendar**

Florence Straw

Born in the same year as her future husband, Florence Anne was the third of David and Elizabeth Winks's five surviving children. She was educated at Dalestorth House, a girls' boarding school near Mansfield.

Teenage years

Florence was a spirited young girl, quick to defend her younger sister Lilian and with a taste for mischief. Her diary for March 1880, when she was 15, records: 'On Wednesday ... we saw two Grammar School boys pass and I knocked at the window and waved my hand-kerchief and they ... took off their hats and I smiled at them and Miss Vallance was cross.' Earlier in the month Florence wrote: 'After dinner went out for a walk and met a man and he was very inquisitive and after tea he came to Dalestorth and Mr G [a teacher] shut the door in his face.'

Outside school, Florence took cookery and sewing classes. She also taught at the local Sunday school. Years later, in 1926, a testimonial from a former student cast light on Florence's nature: 'I am so sorry I was so unkind but I do hope you have forgiven me. Your saying is a very true one, you can-not put [an] old head on young shoulders. You will be pleased to hear I've lost that nasty little temper. I thank you very kindly for the good tuition you gave me ... & I'm grateful to say you have been the making of me.'

Mother and matriarch

Family life was the making of Florence. She doted on her first child William, whom she called 'Babsy'. On holiday with her parents in 1898 she found insufficient supplies of rusks for 'his Lordship', and wrote to her husband: 'I can manage until Monday if you could pack up some in a starch box … our young man is quite a favourite … he has begun to talk … and I am thankful to say … he has been a treat … From your loving wife, Florrie, Kisses from Babsy.'

Florence's scope for home-making above the shop was necessarily limited. It was not until 1920, when the family moved to Endcliffe Villa, that Florence had the chance to decorate in her own style. Papers were chosen from the most up-to-date ranges, along with fashionable parquet linoleum. The Straws also commissioned *trompe l'oeil* decoration, and a fully plumbed bathroom.

One of the last images of Florence was taken on the beach at Scarborough with Walter: a tiny, determined figure whose stamp on her family of men is as evident in Mr Straw's House today as it was the day she died, after a short illness, in November 1939.

Opposite **Florence at Endcliffe Villa**

Above left **The dressing table in Florence's bedroom**

Below left **A sampler made by Florence in 1875**

Baby David

David Harold Straw was born in 1901, the third son of William and Florence. Florence seems to have suffered ill health which necessitated extended holidays, sometimes away from her family. She writes from Scarborough in 1902: 'I feel stronger I am thankful to say, but the last day or two I have not felt so well. It will take time.' William writes back encouragingly on 7 August: 'David comes on wonderful, you will scarcely know him …', but an air of concern pervades their correspondence. David's early promise proved illusory and he died in 1903, aged only two. Infant deaths were still commonplace then, which perhaps explains why this tragedy passed largely unremarked in family annals.

William Straw Jr

William was a strong character who won prizes for academic work throughout his school career. He became a teacher, and from 1921 was assistant master and English teacher at the City of London College, rising to the post of housemaster. In 1937 a dispute over his salary prompted his resignation. He never taught again, and on the death of his mother, returned to Worksop to take up the role of housekeeper at Endcliffe Villa.

William became a local historian and immersed himself in the civic life of the town. He was asked to provide copy for the firm of auctioneers selling the Thorpe Salvin Estate in 1948; he was consulted by the town clerk before the vault of William Edgar Allen, a Sheffield industrialist, was opened; he championed causes he was interested in and served on a number of local committees. He was a member of the Thoroton Society (the society for Nottinghamshire's local historians) and wrote a history of St John's Church in Worksop.

William bought and devoured books, collecting first editions and scarce histories, and almost any available text by or about Shakespeare. He enjoyed a dedicated adherence to correct form (particularly in grammar), and shared his father's love of order and achievement. A relentless recorder of detail, his diary is both mundane: 'bought plastic rain coat 35/-' and profound: 'We buried my dear mother. Horses to hearse, 14 choirboys, 28 wreaths.'

> '*I have no 'wireless' ... because I dislike having my home invaded by people who chatter, shout, sing and from time to time play upon the flute ...*'
>
> William Straw Jr, 8 December 1941

William was never averse to lobbying those in power if he felt moved to do so, particularly on the irritants of modern life such as British Summer Time, to which he was never reconciled (despite recording it faithfully in his diary). As he grew older he became less sociable, retiring behind the net curtains of Endcliffe Villa. However, traditions remained, including his annual autumn bus trip to Nottingham to buy chocolate and other essentials.

William was admitted to hospital in 1985 after falling down the stairs at Endcliffe Villa. He died in December 1990 at the age of 92, having been unable to return to the home that was the private centre of his being.

Opposite **William Jr at the City of London College in the 1920s**

Below **Books from William's bookshelf in his room at Endcliffe Villa**

An antique marble in Worksop

In December 1960 William noticed that the new owner of No. 1 Park Place, around the corner from the shop, was selling a carved marble fragment set into his garden wall. The distressed and distorted naked male torso originated in ancient Pergamon, arriving in suburban Worksop via the London mansion of Lord Arundel (pictured), a Jacobean antiquarian. It had also adorned Worksop Manor, but after this house was sold in 1838, the marble found its way to the home of Robert White, a local historian. William lobbied widely to save the piece. With the help of Mr W.V. Machin of Gateford Hall (whose son remembers William Straw as a forbidding presence), the marble was conveyed to Worksop Library for safe-keeping.

Walter Winks Straw

'[A] very small man, but he always smiled and I can remember his laughter.'

Walter Straw as remembered by Elsie Birch, 2001

Born in 1899, Walter laboured in William's shadow. Although he passed his grocer's exams with distinction in 1920 he deferred to his more academic elder brother. Yet it was he who had the larger front bedroom at Endcliffe Villa, and it is he whom people apparently remember with greater affection.

Walter's year serving in the army during 1918 made use of his grocery skills. He helped to run a military stores on the south coast, where petty theft was a constant concern. He wrote to his mother on 29 March: 'You have to keep [your] eyes on the ration party. A man in a ration party always thinks it is a heaven-sent opportunity for supplementing his own rations.'

On his return to Worksop in 1919 he joined his father in the shop, winning prizes for book-keeping and 'Special Business Methods' from the Institute of Certified Grocers (ICG) in 1922. He taught aspiring grocers at a new college in Worksop and formed a football team from his class, seeking colours for them from the ICG in 1930. He attended the annual conference of the Federation of Grocers' Associations in Blackpool in 1931. His visit to the same conference in Folkestone the following year was curtailed by his father's sudden death.

Walter became President of the Worksop Chamber of Trade and Worksop Grocers' Association in 1954. On 3 March 1962, after 76 years of trading, the shop closed forever. Walter, aged 63, had run the business since his father's death in 1932 and was keen to retire. The property was subsequently rented out.

Walter's many hobbies included growing dahlias and cacti; he propagated the latter in his greenhouse in the back garden. He was also an amateur archaeologist, and helped uncover the remains of the Iron Age settlement at Scratta Wood near Shireoaks. This prompted the formation of the Worksop Society for Archaeological Research, of which Walter was a founding committee member. In 1972 he joined the local committee of the Council for British Archaeology.

Evidently Walter also had an interest in dancing, having subscribed to a correspondence course in dancing lessons from the Arthur Murray School of Dancing in 1924. He died in hospital in Worksop in 1976.

Opposite **Walter in his military uniform in 1918**

Top left **A wall cabinet in Walter's room at Endcliffe Villa**

Top right **Walter (front) with friends in the 1920s**

A cold winter's cactus

The winter of 1939/40 was prolonged and icy, causing havoc in Walter's greenhouse. He shared the details with fellow cacti enthusiasts across the world, sending a letter to the *Journal of the Cactus and Succulent Society of America*: 'On the night of January 20 … the registering therometer [sic] fell to 20 degrees F … A pineapple plant collapsed at once, but the cacti were some time before showing any effects. *Lemaireocereus dumortieri* was the first to go after about a week, and a fortnight later *Ferocactus corniger* turned brown at the top and … became a total loss. *Mammillaria occidentalis* … and *Ferocactus flavovirens* soon followed. I was particularly sorry to lose the last as it was … the spikiest cactus I had. *Lemaireocereus weberi* was also caught, but a surgical operation appears to have saved its life.' He goes on to record more than 300 different varieties in his collection in May 1940.

The Early Years, 1864–1939

The Winks and Straw families were merchants of some distinction in Nottinghamshire.

Walter Straw, William Sr's father, had established the family business manufacturing both house bricks and domestic earthenwares. From red pottery, flower pots and rhubarb forcers, to glazed pancheons and pipkins, he fulfilled much of the demand of the Nottingham and Derbyshire borderlands.

David Winks, William's father-in-law, had an established county butcher's business in Worksop, and was a founding member of the Worksop Traders' Association. With the 'Dukeries' nearby – so named for the number of ducal estates in the area – David's obituarist noted that he was a 'personal friend of the late Duke' (the Duke in question being William John Cavendish-Scott-Bentinck, 5th Duke of Portland, famously reclusive and always more at ease with tradesmen than with his social equals). David disbursed charity to the poorer tenants of both the Dukes of Portland (Welbeck) and Newcastle (Clumber) at Christmas in the form of a joint of beef or mutton.

In 1889, when the young William Straw was establishing his grocery business in the Market Place in Worksop, it was natural that he should look to David Winks, a prominent older citizen

and shopkeeper, for advice. William was also looking for a wife, and found one in the bright and forthright daughter of his mentor.

The business and family thrived in tandem. Three children followed William and Florence's marriage in 1896, while William was able to buy his shop premises, as well as the adjacent property, with help from friends in the trade who shared his interest in gardening. Mr Hillyard, his tea merchant, wrote: 'Should you find this [purchase] ties you up a bit … I shall be happy to give you any extension you like extra & to send you all the tea you want. You will note that the rose trees want pruning. If these do well I will send you a few more … next year. It is always a pleasure to meet a man who loves his garden as I do. Yours truly, N. Hillyard.'

A further major property acquisition was made in 1920 when Endcliffe Villa, on the recently developed private road of Blyth Grove, north of the town centre, came on the market. From 1923 this house became the family home, refurbished using modern conveniences and carefully selected antiques.

Following William's sudden death in 1932, Florence struggled on. William Jr continued to teach in London until 1939, the year Florence died. William then returned from London to join his brother in Worksop, and Mr Straw's House as we know it today was born.

Pottery

Domestic earthenware was the workhorse of the Victorian kitchen. Pancheons – wide, flared bowls – were ideal for a number of roles, including working bread dough, mixing ingredients or setting cream to separate. Other useful earthenware common in kitchens included storage jars, vessels for liquids (pipkins) and tableware such as plates, mugs and dishes, often decorated in cream-coloured glaze trailed over the brown earthenware, in herringbone or spotted patterns.

Above The receipt for the Straws' purchase of Endcliffe Villa in 1920

Top left The Straw family in the early 1900s, in the yard at the back of the shop

Bottom left William and Florence at Endcliffe Villa

Bottom far left Sanderson curtains in the Parlour at Endcliffe Villa

Brothers Alone, 1939–1976

The brothers settled into a new routine after Florence's death. During the war Walter continued to run the shop, while William worked as a labourer at Hall Farm, Ranby, for his cousin Reg Wood.

Diary entries show that William enjoyed the life of a farm labourer. At home he slept in the attic room, while Walter retained the larger front bedroom. Their parents' bedroom remained untouched and unused (except to store William's parcels of books under the bed). Together, bowler-hatted and pinstripe-suited, the brothers went to church each Sunday morning and, changing into trilbies, walked an unvarying afternoon route around the town to inspect their property.

Like their father, the brothers extended their local property empire, responding positively to a message from No. 5 next door in September 1941: 'Miss Beard sent for me, offered to sell her house …' and two days later they 'agreed with [her] to buy at £600 and to let at £36 [annually]'. In November 1949, William 'met L. Seymour at Cattle Market. He offered to sell [some of his] garden for £40 and I agreed to take it at that price.' And a few months later William wrote: 'Walt bought Park St. Gardens on my behalf [for] £380 …'

William continued to buy antiques and books at house sales. At Grove Hall in 1946 he bought *An Historical Account of the Town of Nottingham* by Charles Deering, published in 1751, for £5. Earlier the same year, he bought a prismatic compass (30/-) and a book called *Nottinghamshire and Derbyshire Notes and Queries* (35/-).

William also cultivated his father's allotment and the garden, supplying the home with fruit, vegetables and flowers. On 31 October 1965 he recorded '[the] last boil of beans. 20 Sundays in succession. A record.' He baked bread each week in tiny tins, tended bees and sternly resisted the advance of modern technology (no radio, television or telephone has ever been installed at Endcliffe Villa).

Walter tended his cacti, auriculas and dahlias, and listened to the radio at his cousin's shop in the Market Place. Any further connection the brothers made with technology was limited to their neighbour's telephone. William recorded in his diary: 'BBC phoned no. 9 suggesting … I could appear on television re. Arundel Marbles.

I did not accept.' The Worksop Guardian was the family's main source of news (William had had it sent to him in London every week). In old age, Walter recalled his father's opinion of the wireless: 'Well, I suppose it's alright for people who are ill or who can't read, but I don't think we need one,' adding: 'We've never thought to disagree with him.'

On 16 December 1976 the brothers' harmonious living arrangements came to an end, as William recorded: 'My dear brother Walter Winks Straw died this morning in Kilton Hospital [Worksop].'

Careful housekeeping

Running a thrifty home was second nature to the brothers. Few better illustrations of this survive than the record in William's diary for 5 March 1963: 'Postman tendered open and unstamped packet containing 2 Retfordians [old school magazine]. [H]e claimed 10d (4p) so we refused it.'

Centre The piano in Florence's Parlour, used by the brothers to store books and papers

Far left Walter and William Straw in the 1970s

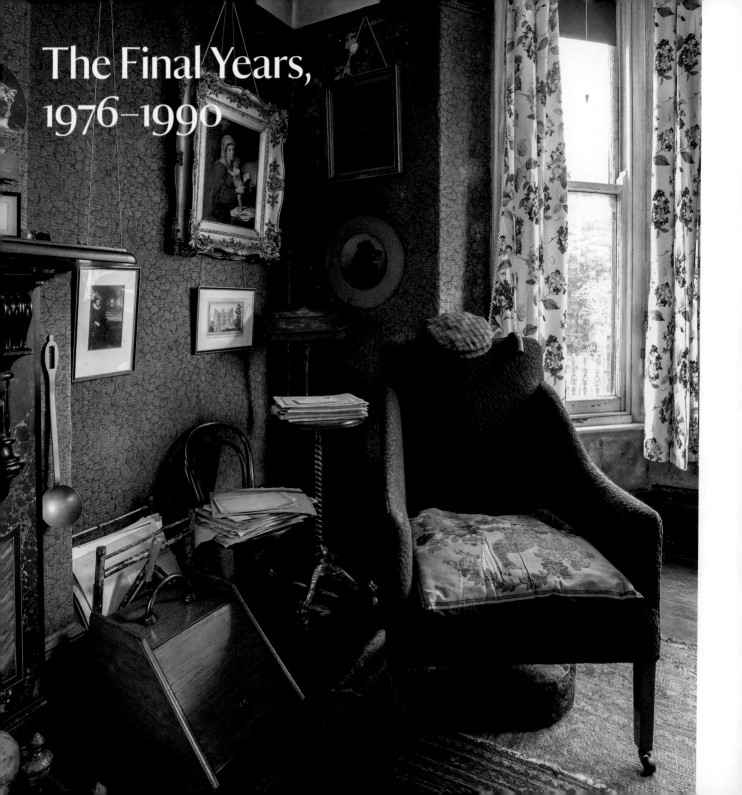

The Final Years,
1976–1990

Following his brother's death William gathered the sentimental remains of his life around him. In his diary for 1977 he records: 'In clearing up the old "Tea Room" at [the] Market Place I found a small Account book … of my uncle Benjamin … [and] I brought away the old hanging Tea Scales.'

Investments provided William with some stability. His father had viewed the arrival of Marks and Spencer in Worksop with trepidation, but decided to buy shares in the rival to hedge against potential loss of trade. As it was a profitable investment his son carried it on, but William Jr refused to shop there, considering the prices 'outrageous'.

Other income came from letting properties in his portfolio. On 11 February 1978 new tenants moved into 5 Blyth Grove, next door to Endcliffe Villa, with their son. A couple of years later, this son took up the tenancy of 9 White Hart, another property owned by William.

Always methodical – even pedantic – in his manner, William preferred books to people, and if people had to visit, he preferred that they did not stay too long. Eric Winks recalled his cousin's distinct coolness if anyone called unexpectedly at a mealtime, when hospitality was seldom offered. These traits became more pronounced with age, and he became increasingly reclusive. In 1984/5, his last at Blyth Grove, anarchy loomed locally, with frequent clashes between miners and police. One can only imagine William's response to the 'Battle of Orgreave', a violent confrontation between police and strikers at a nearby British Steel Corporation coking plant, and the fleets of armoured police vehicles called up in response.

Late in 1985 William fell down the stairs at home and was admitted to the Victoria Hospital in Worksop. There he stayed, keeping in touch with happenings at home via his remaining family and his long-standing tenant at 5 Blyth Grove. He died in December 1990.

A national treasure

William Jr generously bequeathed his property to the National Trust, but it took historic buildings staff six months to persuade their colleagues of the importance of Mr Straw's legacy. The significance of the house – its contents, decoration and garden – is greater than the sum of its parts. Mr Straw's House provides an important social document summing up life in the Midlands of England in the mid-20th century.

Opposite William's chair in the dining room

Left William's wardrobe

Exploring the House

Blyth Grove was developed as a series of speculative and private commissions around the turn of the 20th century.

The pair of semi-detached houses that became Warwick and Endcliffe Villas (Nos 5 and 7) were designed in 1901 by the Worksop-based architect and surveyor, Thomas Webster. Webster's plans superseded that of a detached villa designed in 1898 by T.H. Pennington, but never built.

Webster designed a number of houses locally; he also extended a jam factory in Worksop and built a half-timbered garage in the neighbouring village of Cuckney.

Mirroring each other in layout, the ground floor of Nos 5 and 7 consisted of front and back parlours, a kitchen and an outside store. The cellar had two rooms. Three bedrooms and a bathroom occupied the first floor, with a further two bedrooms and a store in the attic. Bells in the kitchen attest to the original intention of having a servant, although it is doubtful whether any servant ever lived in (as opposed to coming in daily, as the Straws' help did).

After the purchase of No. 7 in 1920, William and Florence redecorated from top to bottom. Local tradesmen were used: Eyre and Sons, a neighbouring business in the Market Place, provided curtains, carpets, linoleum, loose covers and blinds, whilst Pearsons of Eastgate did the painting and papering. Arthur Mallender, a plumber by trade, installed electricity, and Watsons of Potter Street did carpentry work including shelving in the kitchen and extra cupboards in the bathroom. Much of what you see today in the house dates from this interior redecoration.

A few years later the firm of T.J. Green of Watson Road provided a new bath, complete with chrome taps and waste, itemising the cost (£21 11s 11d) on an invoice tinted in the eponymous shade. It is thought-provoking that electricity was installed in this upwardly mobile mercantile household in Worksop in 1923, while 50 miles away at Calke Abbey, one of Derbyshire's great mansions, it took another 40 years for the same amenity to be installed.

An unchanging home

In the years following William and Florence's deaths, change at Mr Straw's House was moderate and followed need rather than fashion. William Jr noted that when the net curtains in the dining room were replaced in 1960, they had previously been renewed in 1936. Over the years he recorded in his diary minor painting and decoration work, and the fixing of a new 'Rutland' grate in the kitchen.

Minor decorative changes aside, the tenor of the house – its ambience and timeless character – did not change. Indeed, as time passed the significance of the unchanging nature of its furnishings came to assume an unparalleled

importance. Here was a carefully preserved and maintained 1920s interior, and yet it had remained the home of two bachelor brothers for six decades thereafter. Commentators have described the brothers as 'living on the surface' of their parents' home, adopting a lifestyle of 'simplicity' and 'frugality'. It seems likely that the innate social conservatism that characterised the boys' upbringing fostered a preference for tradition over innovation. It was not broken, so why change it?

Left The kitchen at Endcliffe Villa

Below The stair carpet reflects the 1920s fashion for all things Egyptian, inspired by the discovery of Tutankhamun's tomb in 1922

More of the same

'More of the same' seems to have been the favoured approach to furnishing the house. Like his father, William Jr bought paintings and furniture at house sales. In 1938 he acquired a watercolour of Edwinstowe by J. Baldock and a brass-bound snakewood writing box, both of which can be seen in the house today.

Elements of the shop found their way back to the house, and added to the décor. Pie moulds and tea canisters decorate a bedroom, while old shop calendars enliven the bedroom corridors.

On the top floor is the Lumber Room and Store Cupboard. William made an inventory of the Store Cupboard in 1941, when food was rationed – not for purposes of hoarding, but as part of his regime of prudent housekeeping. The Lumber Room has more than 2,000 objects in it, including jam jars, war helmets, flags, hot water bottles, seeds, paintings and linen. In a house with extremely limited provision for storage, the Lumber Room reflects the brothers' approach to order, and their ability to look after their family's possessions with great care. It would, however, be unfair to judge this as excessive or unusual: many modern family attics are completely given over to storage, and contain a similarly expansive array of objects and belongings.

Florence's Parlour is a room resonant with her presence: the walls are decorated with the lightest and brightest of her modish wallpapers; the mirrored cabinet contains her trinkets and bibelots, including the photograph of a baby boy (possibly her lost son, David). Yet this room did not freeze at her death – William installed the piano bequeathed to him by his former London landlady at 247 Fulham Road, and added papers, books and biscuit tins from the shop. The boys' parents' bedroom remained unoccupied after their deaths but was never unused – special clothes were kept on the bed, and the cavity under it was used to store books.

A little list…

Inventories appealed to the Straws' love of order. Lists and labels abound; the most informative of the latter are affixed to articles and note their history. The child's rocking chair in William's own bedroom has a label under the seat recording the date of its local manufacture and its provenance as a gift to Florence from her grandmother. Florence's own hand is identified on the back of an embroidered sampler she worked in her schooldays which hangs in the Parlour. The archive is littered with scribbled lists of plants and seeds (often cacti, in Walter's cramped but distinctive hand), books (in William's) and notes on genealogies of local families.

Opposite The Lumber Room, home to a vast collection of objects dating from the 1920s onwards

Above Storage under William and Florence's bed

The garden

Asphalt paths to front and rear are typical of gardens of this scale and vintage. The borders in the back garden have a classic cottage planting scheme of delphiniums, foxgloves, paeonies and chrysanthemums, raised to a slightly more exotic level by the presence of a fig tree and the occasional succulent in a pot, a summer refugee from the greenhouse. The present greenhouse is a precise reproduction of Walter's, which blew down in a storm in the early 1980s.

Passion and pragmatism

Seeds, which were sold in the shop from 1898 until it closed in 1962, were a commercially successful offering which reflected William Sr's own interests. William's allotment off Sparken Hill provided a space to cultivate vegetables and flowers for his home, and somewhere for his growing family to enjoy the summer sun in respectable privacy. It also sowed the seeds of a lifelong interest in gardening for the two young Straw brothers.

For William Jr gardening was part of his daily life once he returned to Worksop in 1939. Its purpose, for him, was to provide fruit and vegetables for the house. A few flowers were permitted, but the main aim was to feed the household.

Walter's passion was for cacti, auriculas and dahlias. This is not to say that he lacked an interest in other flowers – he sold seeds for many varieties in the shop – but his personal interest was very focused. He kept a cactus diary for a few years in the 1930s. On 25 May 1937 he

THE

CACTUS

JOURNAL

Vol. 7   June, 1939   No. 4

CONTENTS

PAGE

Description of *Conophytum*, by Mrs. Louisa Bolus   97

An Experiment in Hybridisation with A. Myriostigma, by
Robert Gräser   103

Cactus Surgery, by the Rev. F. C. Champion   104

" Plantae succulentae, in Horto Alenconio, Auctore H. A.
Duval. Parisiis apud Gabon et Socios, 1809 "   105

Growing Stapelias, by S. G. Fiedler   110

113

'We have been called a nation of shopkeepers; we might with equal justice be called a nation of gardeners.'

William Straw, 1 June 1939

recorded potting 20 cacti, followed by an entry two days later: 'finished potting … making a very nice display'. He wrote about both triumphs, such as on 12 September 1938: '*Coryph elephantidens* in bloom. Opened daily to 15th …' and disasters, such as that on 6 July 1939: 'Found *Echinocereus rufispinum* had rotted at root. Cut off & set to dry. *Echinomartus* … also has shrivelled up.' He was innovative: '[22 April 1938] Cacti arrived from T. Schmoll, Mexico', although not always careful: '[23 April 1938] letter from Ministry of Agr. re. import of cacti'. He was regarded as an authority, and was sent seeds for trial by seed merchants.

In the front garden, spring and summer bedding plants enlivened the otherwise stark square of lawn bounded by a privet hedge. The strange appearance of the mulberry tree is the result of pruning damage inflicted, possibly, towards the end of William Jr's life. Using land which came with the house, the garden at No. 7 was expanded into an allotment across the road (now the visitors car park). This was set out by William Jr as an orchard, and a few trees still survive.

Clockwise from top right
Walter's cacti diary from 1930; *The Cactus Journal* from 1939 – front cover and interior illustrations; William's hand-drawn plan for the orchard in what is now the visitors car park; William Sr, in a bowler hat, with family and friends

Keeping House

Like a suburban iceberg, only a small part of the collection in Mr Straw's House is actually visible.

The majority of items – the everyday props of an ordered household of the pre-digital age, including paper clips, envelopes, string and elastic bands, as well as several generations of the family's clothes and domestic necessities, from tablecloths to jam jars, and clothes pegs to garden canes – are all stored in drawers, cupboards and under beds.

Challenges of conservation

The rooms of Mr Straw's House contain one of the largest inventories of chattels of any property in the National Trust. This presents special challenges for the care of the collection, and for the preservation of Florence's meticulous decorations. There is no space large enough in the property to lay out some of the larger items of clothing, which makes checking for pests and cleaning a challenge. Just getting into the corners of every room to clean requires careful removal of contents and then equally careful and precise replacement. Precision is vital in a property where authenticity lies in the arrangement of the interiors.

A small team of dedicated employees and volunteers welcome thousands of visitors into this semi-detached house each year. The effect on the fabric from such an influx is so much greater than ordinary domestic wear and tear that the Trust has had to reproduce the stair and corridor carpets, preserving the originals as museum objects. If visitors are asked to refrain from leaning on the wallpaper or scuffing the paintwork, it is only because Mr Straw's House is a delicate survival that must pass on to the next generation, and to the one after that.

Above The volume of everyday mid-20th century objects contained in Mr Straw's House presents staff and volunteers with particular conservation challenges